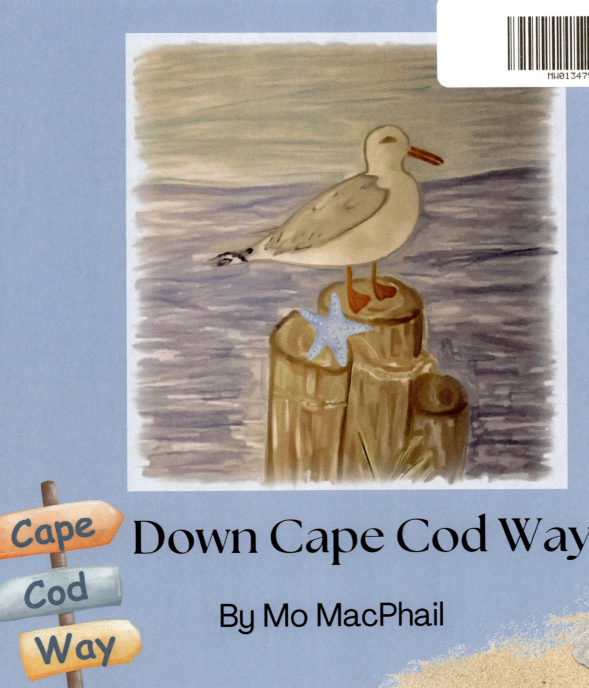

Down Cape Cod Way

By Mo MacPhail

Copyright © 2024 Mo MacPhail

All rights reserved. No part of this book may be used or reproduced by any means, graphic, electronic, or mechanical, including photocopying, retrieval system without the written permission of the author except in the case of brief quotations embodied in critical articles and reviews.

    Come to a special place where the ocean meets the sky, and the air is filled with salty sea spray and the sound of seagulls calling.

    You'll find this beauty **Down Cape Cod Way!**

    A magical place where sandcastles, swimming, sailing, and collecting seashells on the beach are just a few of the favorites for those who visit.

    You can even see whales and dolphins playing in the waves!

    Down Cape Cod Way illustrates the magic you'll find while visiting beautiful Cape Cod, Massachusetts.

Down Cape Cod Way
where the beach plums grow,

Back to the bridge
we'll always go,
for when we do
the seagull will say...

"Come with me and play
in the ocean spray,"
Down Cape Cod Way.

Down Cape Cod Way
where the summer winds blow,

Back to the dunes
we'll always go,
for when we do
the seagull will say...

"Let's go see some whales splash their mighty tails," Down Cape Cod Way.

Down Cape Cod Way
where the rain makes bows,

Back to the waves
we'll always go,
for when we do
the seagull will say...

"Come and see the place
where the sun shines on our face,"
Down Cape Cod Way.

Down Cape Cod Way where the lighthouse glows,

Back to the dock
we'll always go,
for when we do
the seagull will say…

"Let's get on a boat,
far away we'll float,"
Down Cape Cod Way.

Down Cape Cod Way
where the Wild Rose grows,

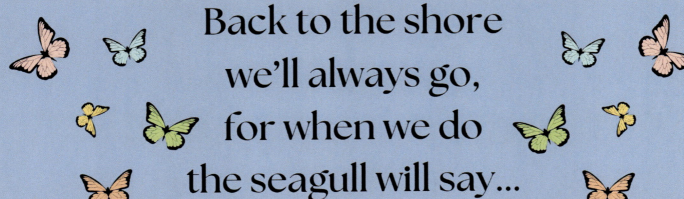

Back to the shore
we'll always go,
for when we do
the seagull will say...

"Let's go find some shells
and paint them with pastels,
Down Cape Cod Way.

Down Cape Cod Way
where Hydrangea grow,

Back to our town
we'll always go,
for when we do
the seagull will say...

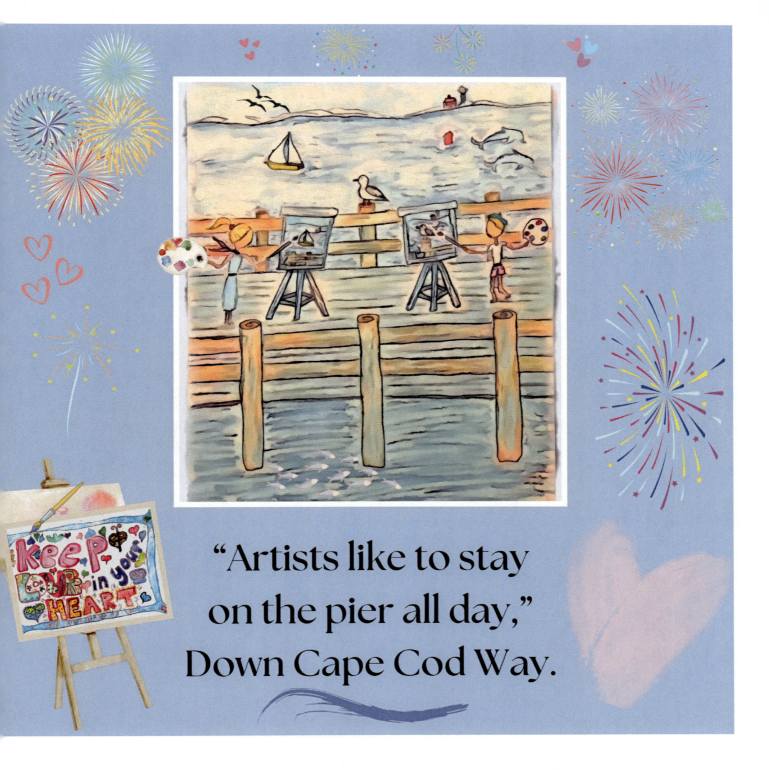

"Artists like to stay on the pier all day," Down Cape Cod Way.

Down Cape Cod Way
where sand gets on your toes,

Back to our chairs
we'll always go,
for when we do
the seagull will say...

"Behind the Osprey nest
the sunset is the best,"
Down Cape Cod Way.

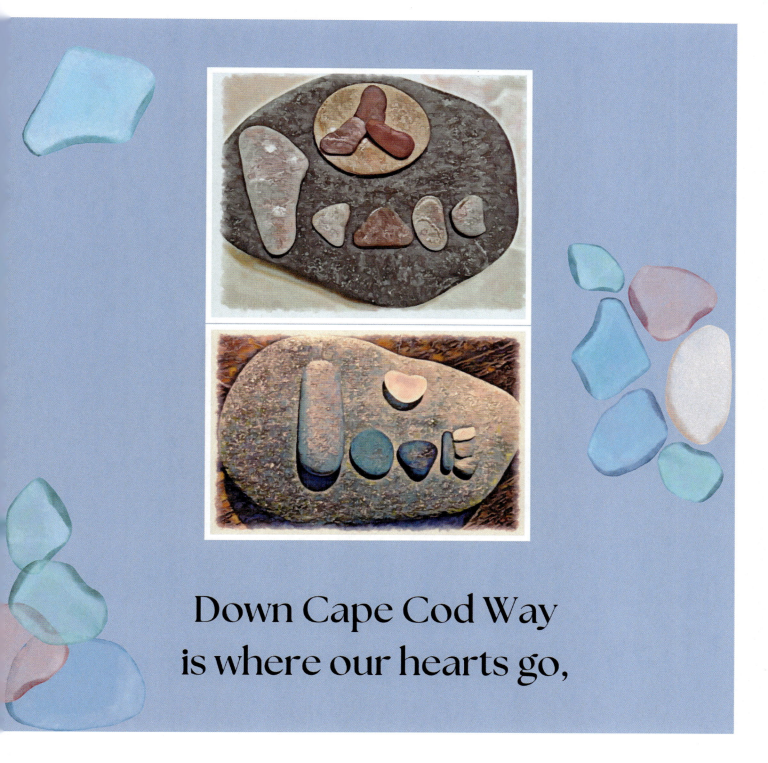

Down Cape Cod Way
is where our hearts go,

Back where the love
will always flow,
for when it does
the seagull will say...

"Let's play with our friends and never let it end," Down Cape Cod Way!

Made in the USA
Middletown, DE
17 December 2024

67535932R10018